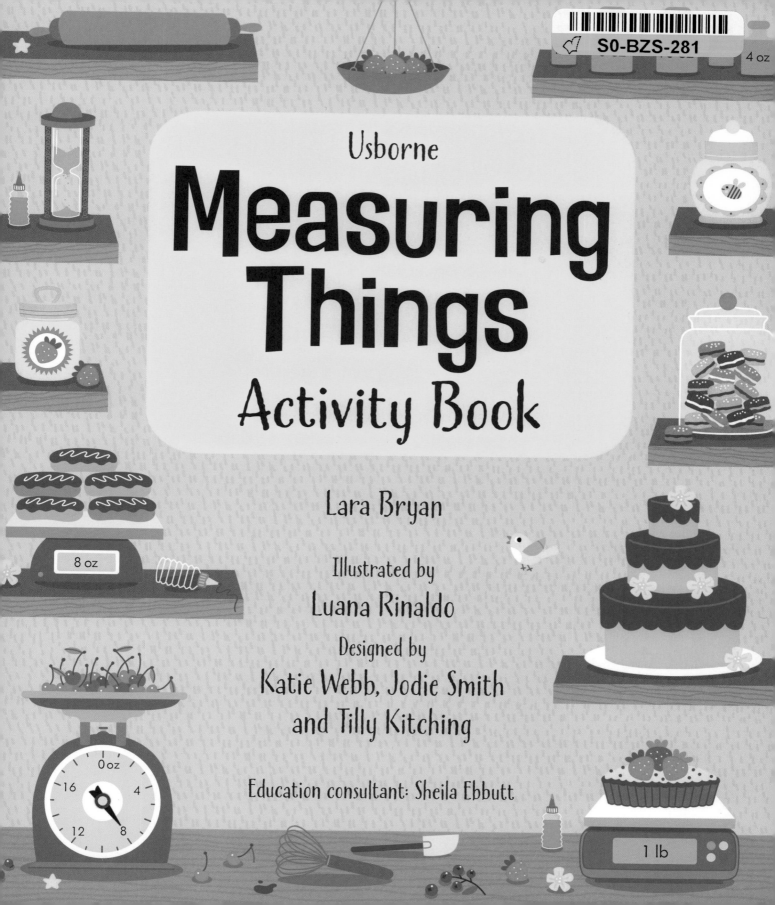

Usborne
Measuring Things
Activity Book

Lara Bryan

Illustrated by
Luana Rinaldo

Designed by
Katie Webb, Jodie Smith
and Tilly Kitching

Education consultant: Sheila Ebbutt

About measuring

People often describe things using words such as big, small, heavy, light, cold, and hot — but those words aren't very precise.

I ran for a long time!

How long?

It can help to compare things to something else.

How tall is this cake?

Twice as tall as this one.

To be more precise, you can measure things using numbers and **units** — agreed amounts that are always the same. That way, everyone knows *what* you're measuring and exactly *how much* you mean.

Common units include feet, pounds and gallons.

This plant is eight feet tall.

That's one foot taller than last week!

There are two main systems of units: **customary** and **metric**.

Customary units are used for everyday measurements in the United States. Most of the units in this book are customary units.

Metric units are often used in science, and in most other countries around the world. Find out more on pages 46–47.

How to use this book

This book is full of activities to help you practice measuring things. It is split into five sections.

Length: pages 4–15

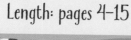

Discover how to measure how tall...

...or small something is!

Perimeter and area: pages 16–23

Perimeter means the distance around the edge of a shape.

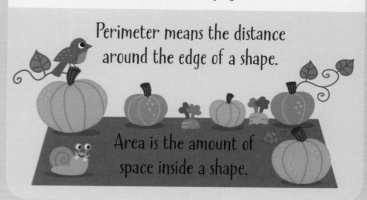

Area is the amount of space inside a shape.

Volume and mass: pages 24–37

Volume means how much space a solid shape takes up.

Mass tells you how heavy something is. You measure it by weighing.

1 lb

More units: pages 38–49

Other things you may need to measure...

Time   Temperature   Turns

More practice: pages 50–57

This section contains extra practice for all kinds of measuring.

Don't worry if you get stuck. Just turn to the answer pages at the back of this book.

Quick Quizzes let you check what you've learned so far. Give yourself a star from the sticker pages for each quiz you complete.

Comparing things

If you want to know how big something is, you can compare one thing to another. You can do this roughly just by guessing or 'estimating'.

It helps if you compare the thing you're measuring to something familiar.

For example:

The circus tent looks about three times as tall as me.

Can you help the clown and his dog put on a hat and bow tie using the stickers from the sticker pages?

My hat is half the height of yours.

My bow tie is twice as wide as yours.

Length is the distance between two points. You can use your handspan to help you estimate lengths.

A handspan is the length from your thumb to your little finger.

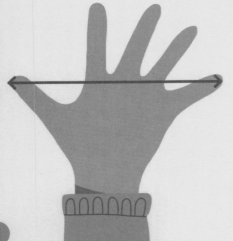

Measure the length of these parts of your body using your handspan.

Length of your face

about .... handspans

Length of your arm, from wrist to shoulder

about .... handspans

Measuring length

To measure length accurately, you need units.
For small lengths, you can use inches.
Inches can be shortened to 'in' or ".

Each of these seeds is 1 inch apart.

1 in

For smaller lengths, you can use
half inches, quarter inches
or even eighths.

Yum!

$\frac{1}{2}$ in $\frac{1}{4}$ in $\frac{1}{8}$ in

You can measure lengths using a ruler.

Line up one
end with zero.

Read the length
at this end.

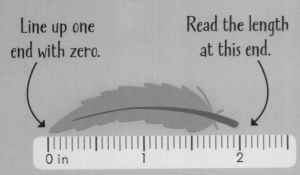

0 in   1   2

Each big line on the ruler is one inch and the
smaller ones are fractions of inches. So this
feather is two inches long.

Using a ruler, can you help the naturalist
measure these creatures?

....

....

....

....

Be as accurate
as you can!

....

These birds are collecting twigs for their nest.
How long do you think the shortest twig is?
And the longest? Then measure them with a ruler
to see how close you were.

Shortest: ....   Longest: ....

How long is the caterpillar? ....

One week later — how long is it now? ....

About how many inches does each frog have to jump to reach the lily pads in the middle? Estimate first, then measure to check your answer.

....

....

Starting from this flower, stick a flower from the sticker pages at every inch until there are five flowers in the planter. Use a ruler to help you.

How accurate?

Sometimes, the thing you're measuring might not line up exactly with a marking. In this case, just choose the closest. For most everyday measurements, measuring to the nearest eighth of an inch is accurate enough.

If you don't have a ruler, you could cut out this one. It has inches on this side and centimeters on the other.

0 in
Remember always to start measuring from 0.
1
2
3
4
5
6
7
8
9

Longer distances

To measure longer lengths you can use feet (ft) and yards (yd). There are 12 inches in a foot and 3 feet in a yard.

1 ft is roughly the length of a step.

← 1 ft → ← 1 yd →

For even longer distances you can use miles (mi). There are 1,760 yd or 5,280 ft in a mile.

That's about the distance you'd run in 15 minutes.

Using suitable units means the numbers don't get too big.

BEACH →
8 km 5 miles

In some countries, you might see distances in kilometers (km). 1 mile is roughly 1.6 km.

Remember always to start measuring from 0.

Can you circle the units you would use to measure these distances?

A sailing trip around the world
yd / mi

Length of a beach towel
ft / mi

Height of an umbrella
ft / mi

The orange sail is 4 yd high. Roughly how high is the small sail?

....

These children are competing to build the longest sandcastle. Look at the tape measures to find the length of each one, then stick a ribbon from the sticker pages on the longest.

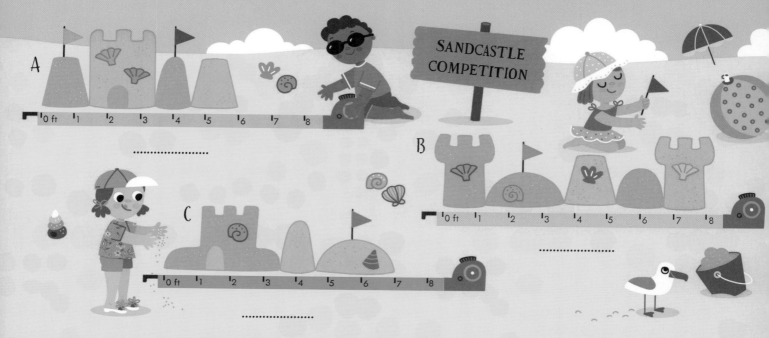

This surfer needs a surfboard about 2 ft taller than she is. Look at the measuring stick on the left and work out the one she needs, then color it in.

Miles are too big to measure without special equipment. But you can get a good idea by roughly guessing. For example, it takes about 15 minutes to run 1 mile. Roughly how far have these runners run?

We've been running for just over 7 minutes.

So we've run about ...... mi.

From one unit to another

Here's how to change between units:

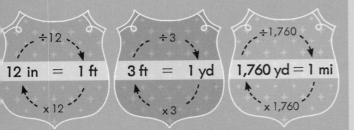

÷12	÷3	÷1,760
12 in = 1 ft	3 ft = 1 yd	1,760 yd = 1 mi
x 12	x 3	x 1,760

Converting units is helpful if the numbers are getting too big or too small.

My tower is 0.0049 mi high.

It's simpler to say the tower is 26 ft high.

Converting is also useful if the measurements you're working with aren't all in the same unit. How tall is this suit of armor?

Helmet
= 12 in
= 1 ft

So the total height is:
1 + 5 = 6 ft

Body
= 5 ft

Just big enough for me.

Can you draw a line between the same distances?

1 yd	1 ft
12 in	4 yd
6 ft	2 yd
12 ft	3 ft

Put an X by the goblets of the same height and the plates of the same width.

Gold goblet: 6 in ☐
Silver goblet: $\frac{1}{2}$ ft ☐
Bronze goblet: $\frac{1}{4}$ ft ☐

Emerald plate: $1\frac{1}{2}$ ft ☐
Copper plate: 15 in ☐
Ruby plate: 18 in ☐

Help the princess find a route through the maze. How long is her route?

The queen has boasted she owns 10 ft of necklaces. Is it true?

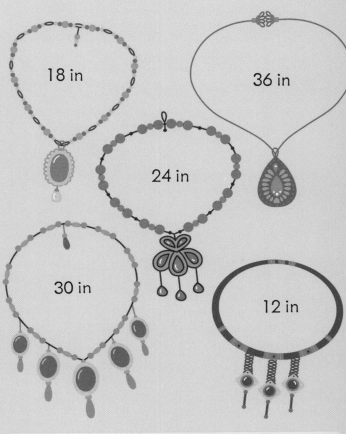

18 in

36 in

24 in

30 in

12 in

.... yd

Is that more or less than one mile?   MORE / LESS

Use this space for working out.

.... in = ... ft

These birds are delivering messages to the places on the signpost. Can you write each of their destinations onto the messages?

2 mi ....

600 ft ....

$\frac{1}{2}$ mi ....

Castle 3,520 yd

Inn 880 yd

House 200 yd

These riders are getting onto their horses. Can you estimate how high it is from the ground to the top of each saddle? The first one has been done for you.

The saddle looks twice as high as my mounting block. So it is about 3 ft high.

3 ft

1½ ft

2 ft

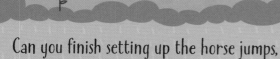

.... ft

1 ft

.... ft

Can you finish setting up the horse jumps, following the instructions?

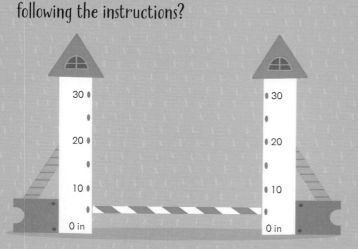

30

20

10

0 in

30

20

10

0 in

Draw on extra horizontal poles between the towers, every 10 in up from the bottom pole.

Each hay bale is 25 in high. Add sticker hay bales to make the jump 75 in high.

12

Can you measure the lengths of these jumps and write the answers below?
Then, stick three riders onto the horses, following the clues on the sign.

CLUES

The red rider's jump is 2 ft longer than the blue rider's jump, and ½ ft longer than the green rider's jump.

Lengths of the jumps

A) ....

B) ....

C) ....

Can you put these lines in order by comparing them?

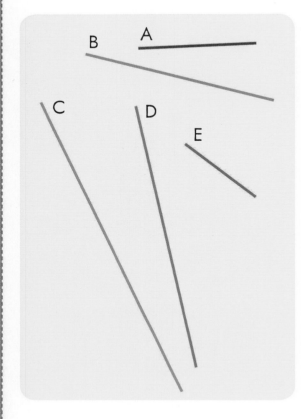

Longest ....

↓

....

....

....

Shortest ....

Score

_____

5

Sticker

Can you match each measuring device to the correct description?

1) Can be used to measure large objects, such as furniture. One end has a metal hook to help keep it in place while you measure. ....

2) Can be used to measure small objects, such as the lines on a page. ....

3) Can be used to measure curved things, such as your waist. ....

A) Ruler

B) Measuring tape

C) Tape measure

Score

_____

3

Sticker

14

Which unit would you use to measure these lengths?

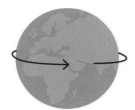

Distance around the world.

....

Height of a house

....

Length of a slug

....

Length of a pair of jeans

....

Score

Sticker

4

Convert these units.

1 yd = ... ft

1 ft = ... in

9 ft = ... yd

48 in = ... ft

$\frac{1}{3}$ yd = ... ft

2 ft = ... in

10 yd = ... ft

1 mi = ... yd

$\frac{1}{2}$ ft = ... in

Score

Sticker

9

Perimeter

The distance around the outside edge of a shape is called its **perimeter**.

To find a shape's perimeter, measure the length of its sides and then add them up.

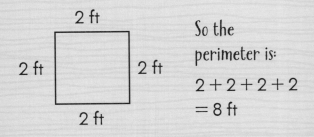

2 ft

2 ft   2 ft

2 ft

So the perimeter is:

2 + 2 + 2 + 2 = 8 ft

Who has got the perimeter right?

We'll need 40 yd of wire to go around the chicken coop.

No, we'll need 30 yd.

10 yd

5yd   Coop plans   5 yd

10 yd

The farmer is going to dig a trench around each vegetable patch. How far does she need to dig for each?

.... yd

1 yd

.... yd

3 yd

2 yd

3 yd

2 yd   3 yd   3 yd

3 yd

5 yd

2 yd

2 yd

1 yd

.... yd

5 yd

Use this space for any working out.

This sheep pen is a rectangle 25 yd long and 15 yd wide. Which sheepdog has just run around the perimeter to check for missing sheep?

I've run 50 yd.

I've run 80 yd.

I've run 30 yd.

Use this space for any working out.

Help the farmer mark out a fence around the geese by linking the dots following the numbers 1 to 11. The first line, between 1 and 2, has been done for you.

The distance between each dot on the grid is 1 yd. How many yards of fencing will the farmer need? ....

Area

The amount of space that a flat shape takes up is called its **area**.

A square with sides of one inch has an area of one inch *squared* – written as 1 in².

1 in

1 in = 1 in²

The little '2' means squared.

To find the area of a shape, you can count how many squares fit inside it.

This rectangle contains six squares. Each square is 1 in², so the area is 6 in².

You can also use squares to help you estimate the area of irregular shapes. If a square is more than half full, count it as one square. If it is less than half full, don't count it.

This rocket has an area of about 4 in².

1 in

1 in

Can you estimate the area of these irregular shapes?

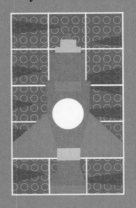

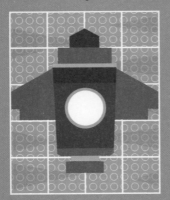

Each little square on these pages stands for 1 in².

Can you work out the area of these alien characters and then color them in, following the key?

16 in²   13 in²   21 in²

....

....

....

....

In this game, the aim is to help the spaceship make its deliveries. Work out the area of each planet, then follow the key below to add the right sticker to each planet.

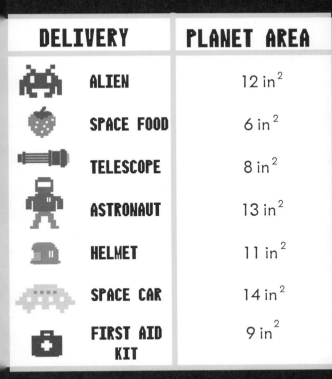

DELIVERY		PLANET AREA
	ALIEN	12 in^2
	SPACE FOOD	6 in^2
	TELESCOPE	8 in^2
	ASTRONAUT	13 in^2
	HELMET	11 in^2
	SPACE CAR	14 in^2
	FIRST AID KIT	9 in^2

For each planet the spaceship visits, it wins a badge.

Can you work out which badges this spaceship has won, and stick them on below?

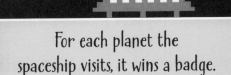

PLANET	REWARD
Area up to 10 in^2	
Area from 11 to 20 in^2	

More area

Counting squares to work out the area of a shape can take a while. If you have a rectangle or square, it's faster to multiply the number of rows by the number of columns, like this...

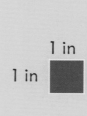

1 in

1 in

4 columns

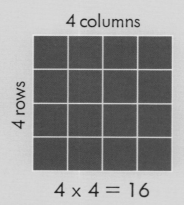

4 rows

$4 \times 4 = 16$

So the area of this shape is 16 in^2.

Fill in the area of these gingerbread houses.

$10 \times \ldots\ldots = \ldots\ldots$ in^2

$9 \times \ldots\ldots = \ldots\ldots$ in^2

$\ldots\ldots \times \ldots\ldots = \ldots\ldots$ in^2

How many candy roof tiles?

....

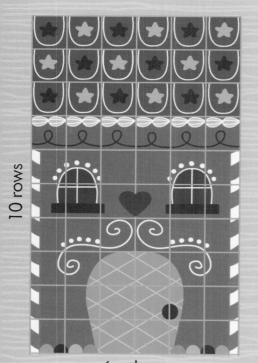

10 rows

6 columns

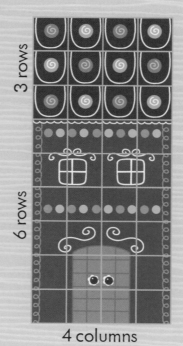

3 rows

6 rows

4 columns

8 rows

8 columns

Give this house a door and windows from the sticker pages. What's their total area?

Window area = ...

Window area = ...

Door area = ...

Total = ... in^2

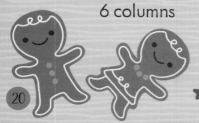

What was the area of this piece of candy *before* the bakers cut out three roof tiles from it?

.... x .... = ... in²

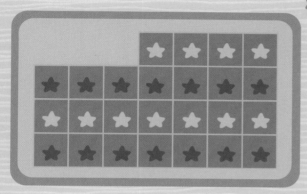

You can break some irregular shapes down into rectangles, to help calculate their area.

To work out the area of the whole castle, first work out the area of each tower.

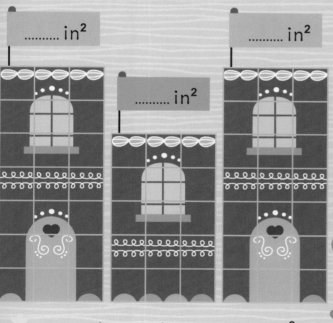

.... in²   .... in²

.... in²

.... + ... + ... = ... in²

This is a fresh piece of gingerbread. Roughly how many gingerbread men of this size do you think could be cut from it?

.... gingerbread men

Can you spot a gingerbread house that is twice the area of this one?

Gingerbread Street

Use this space for working out.

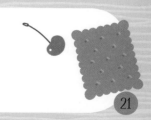

What is the perimeter of these shapes?

A)

4 in

4 in   4 in

4 in

....

B)

2.5 in

2 in

3 in

7 in

3 in

3 in

2 in

2.5 in   ....

Score   Sticker

_____
2

How far is it around the edge of this field?

25 yd

50 yd

....

What is the perimeter of a square vegetable patch with 5 yd sides?

....

A rectangular field has a long edge of 100 yd and a short edge of 50 yd. What is its perimeter?

....

Score   Sticker

_____
3

Each of the little squares on this page represents 1 in².

Find the area of these shapes.

A)
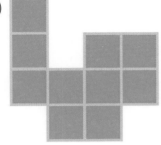

B)
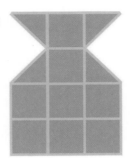

C)
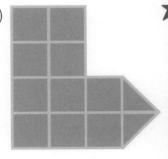

....

....

....

Can you roughly *estimate* the area of this shape?

Tip: don't count squares that are less than half full. Count squares that are half full or more as a whole.

....

D)
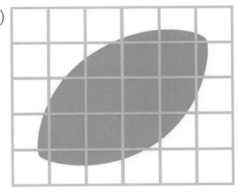

Can you find the area of the irregular shape, by adding the areas of the two rectangles?

E)
2 in   2 in

3 in
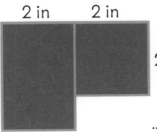
2 in

.... + ...

= ....

Score

_____

5

Sticker

23

Capacity

Capacity is the amount a container can hold.

You can fit four sugar cubes into this box, so that's its capacity.

Words like 'full' and 'empty' describe how much of a container's capacity has been filled. Match the sticker jars to each mouse.

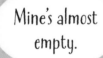

My jar is full.

Mine's almost empty.

My jar is half full.

Can you estimate which of these containers has the biggest capacity, and which has the smallest?

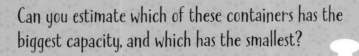

Honey

Peanut Butter

Strawberry Jelly

Maple Syrup

Spread

Hands-on measuring

Find a big container, such as a saucepan, and a cup, and try the following.

How many cups of water does it take to...

....half fill the big container?

.... cups

....completely fill it?

.... cups

Volume

Volume is the amount of space something takes up. You can use units of volume to measure capacity.

One way of measuring volume is with cubes.

This cube has a height, width and depth of 1 in. So its volume is one inch *cubed* – written as 1 in³.

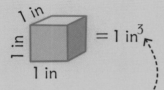

The little '3' means cubed.

To find the volume of a bigger block, you can work out the number of cubes that fit inside it.

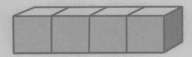

This block is made up of four cubes. If each cube is 1 in³, the block has a volume of 4 in³.

This mouse eats three cubes of cheese a day. How many days will each block last?

.... days   .... days   .... days

All these piles of cheese had a volume of four cubes to begin with. Circle the one the mouse stole a cube from.

The mouse with the most cubes of cheese has brown fur. The other one has black fur. Can you color them in?

Volume = ... cubes
= .... in³

Volume = ... cubes
= .... in³

Volume of liquids

To measure the volume of liquids you can use fluid ounces (fl. oz), cups, pints (pt), quarts (qt) and gallons (gal).

$\frac{1}{2}$ fl. oz — 1 cup — $1\frac{1}{2}$ cup

This bottle holds 1 quart of juice.

There are 8 fluid ounces in a cup, 2 cups in a pint, 2 pints in a quart and 4 quarts in a gallon.

You can use this 'volume wall' to see how different volumes compare.

gallon							
quart		quart		quart		quart	
pint	pint	pint	pint	pint	pint	pint	pint
cup cup	cup cup	cup cup	cup cup	cup cup	cup cup	cup cup	cup cup

Hands-on measuring

Look around your home and try and guess the volume of some everyday things. Then check your guess against the label.

Item	Guessed volume	Actual volume
Toothpaste		
Shampoo		
Milk carton		
Oil bottle		

Each dropper contains one cup of liquid. How many will I need to fill each container?

Measuring containers are often marked in pints, cups and ounces.

I've got 12 fl. oz of liquid.

To read the markings, first work out what each mark represents.

Here, the longer marks are every 4 fl. oz or ½ cup. So the marks halfway between represent 2 fl. oz or ¼ cup.

So here there is 6 fl. oz of liquid or ¾ cup.

Can you shade in these test tubes so they are filled to the correct levels?

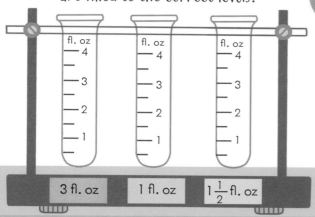

3 fl. oz   1 fl. oz   1 ½ fl. oz

Find the right labels for these flasks from the sticker pages.

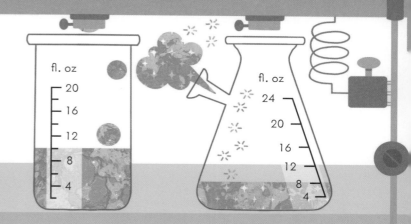

Can you help the scientist fill in her list of ingredients?
Read the amounts on the containers and fill in the blanks.

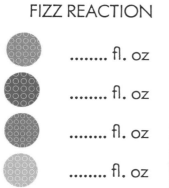

FIZZ REACTION

.... fl. oz

.... fl. oz

.... fl. oz

.... fl. oz

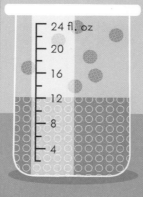

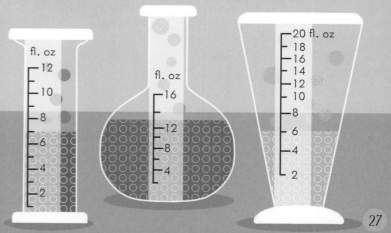

More practice

The workers at the juice factory are developing a new blend of rainbow juice. Can you help them to get it ready?

I need 2 cups of strawberry juice. How much *more* should I add?

....

This machine has 5 cups of kiwi juice to dispense. If each carton holds 8 fl. oz, how many cartons can it fill? Stick on the right number of cartons from the sticker pages.

— 5 cups

I need 4 pints of blueberry juice. How many bottles is that?

2 cups 2 cups 2 cups 2 cups 2 cups 2 cups

.... bottles

Use this space for any working out.

How many pineapple chunks are in each dish? Which pile has the largest volume?

....

Roughly how many ladles of blackberry juice do you think will fill the green pot?

Estimate: .... ladles

Which container has the most mango juice?

4 cups

2

4 cups

2

RAINBOW JUICE

Follow the recipe and color in the right amount of juice in each container.

~ Recipe ~
3 cups of blueberry juice
2½ cups of kiwi juice
12 fl. oz of strawberry juice
18 fl. oz of mango juice

fl. oz	cups	fl. oz	cups	fl. oz	cups	fl. oz	cups
40 — 5		40 — 5		40 — 5		40 — 5	
32 — 4		32 — 4		32 — 4		32 — 4	
24 — 3		24 — 3		24 — 3		24 — 3	
16 — 2		16 — 2		16 — 2		16 — 2	
8 — 1		8 — 1		8 — 1		8 — 1	

Mmmm, fruity!

Measuring mass

The amount of stuff or 'matter' something contains is its **mass**.

To measure the mass of light things you can use ounces (oz).

$$\frac{1}{10} oz \qquad 5 oz$$

The mass of heavier things is measured in pounds (lb).

16 oz = 1 lb

2 lb

Really heavy things can be measured in tons (t).

2,000 lb = 1 t

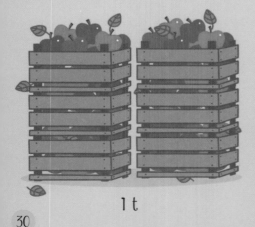

1 t

Circle the correct answers.

How much can an eagle carry in its claws?
4 lb / 4 t

What's the mass of a brown bear?
1,000 lb / 1,000 t

What's the mass of a rabbit?
4 oz / 4 lb

You can't always tell how heavy something will be just from its size. For example, who is carrying the greatest mass?

Our bags are the same size, but I'm carrying all the tools...

...and I've got all the sweaters...

...so my bag is heavier!

These campers are making stew. Read the recipe, then circle the correct amount of each ingredient.

Camper's stew

- 12 oz carrots
- 2 lb potatoes
- 24 oz chicken
- 28 oz canned tomatoes

20 oz

3 lb

16 oz   16 oz

14 oz   14 oz   14 oz   14 oz

Is this cable car strong enough to carry the whole family?

YES / NO

Max 1 ton

Max 1 ton

Cable car ride

130 lb   80 lb   60 lb   160 lb

MASS or WEIGHT?

People often talk about measuring 'weight' in pounds and ounces, rather than 'mass'.

Weight means how strongly gravity is pulling on something, and it is measured in Newtons. (Gravity is the force which pulls everything down on Earth.)

However, gravity doesn't vary much on Earth, so people don't usually worry about Newtons.

This has a weight of 8 lb. Oops, I meant mass!

It's ok, I know what you meant.

8 lb

Using scales

To measure ounces and pounds you use scales.

These scales work by balancing.

These muffins have a mass of ¼ lb.

You add weights to the empty pan until both pans are level.

This set of scales has a moving pointer.

These cookies have a mass of 6 oz.

The pointer moves around to point to the mass of the objects in the pan.

This set of scales is electronic. It displays the mass on the screen.

This quiche has a mass of 1 pound.

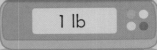

1 lb

The baker has measured out the correct amount of each ingredient. Can you fill in his recipe?

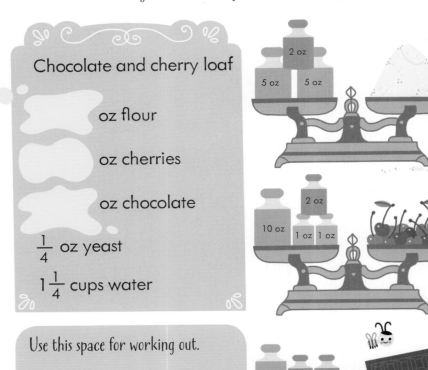

Chocolate and cherry loaf

_____ oz flour

_____ oz cherries

_____ oz chocolate

$\frac{1}{4}$ oz yeast

$1\frac{1}{4}$ cups water

Use this space for working out.

This baker is making raspberry frosting. Can you write the mass of the three piles of raspberries under each set of scales?

It takes 4 oz of dough to make a croissant. How many could you make from this dough? Stick the right number of croissants on the tray.
Tip: 1 lb = 16 oz

$1\frac{1}{2}$ lb

This giant pretzel has a mass of 1 lb. Can you circle the weights needed to make the pans balance?

3 oz

1 oz

2 oz

5 oz

2 oz

5 oz

8 oz

2 oz

This is a 1¼ lb cake.
Can you draw the pointer on the scales?

0 lb
$\frac{1}{2}$
1
$1\frac{1}{2}$
2
$2\frac{1}{2}$
3
$3\frac{1}{2}$
4
$4\frac{1}{2}$

Can you look at the scales and work out these masses?

1 tart: .... lb
4 tarts: .... lb

1 eclair: .... oz
10 eclairs: .... oz or .... lb

2 lb

$1\frac{1}{2}$ lb

Help the vet record the mass of each lion cub.

Ari

Leo

Fluffy

Tuesday March 18
Lion cub weigh-in

Ari: .... lb

Leo: .... lb

Fluffy: .... lb

When this elephant was born, it had a mass of 200 pounds. Now, it is three times as heavy. Can you draw the pointer on these scales?

What's the difference in mass between these baby monkeys?

.... lb = ... oz

$6\frac{1}{2}$ lb

8 lb

34

The mother giraffe has a mass of 1 ton. Her baby is about half her mass. How much is that?

.... lb

Can you help the vet spot the record with the wrong mass written on it?

Hippo
Mass: 14 lb

Antelope
Mass: 56 lb

Leopard
Mass: 70 lb

Each baby meerkat has a mass of about 4 oz. Can you stick the right number of babies onto the scales?

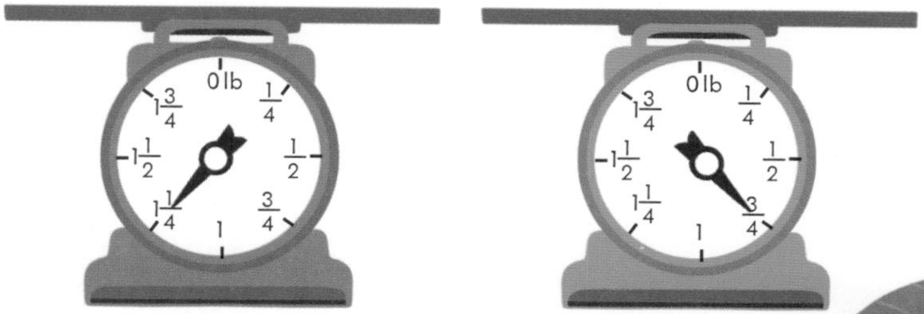

The food for the animals is being measured out. The heavier the animal, the more food it needs. Can you stick the correct animal label onto each of the buckets?

14 lb

196 lb

14 oz

Label these containers 1 to 5, with 1 having the biggest capacity and 5 the smallest.

 ....

 ....

 ....

 ....

 ....

Score

Sticker

_____
5

Each cube has a volume of 1 in³. What is the volume of each pile?

 ....

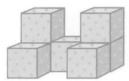 ....

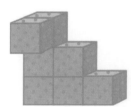 ....

Shade these containers in, to show how full they should be.

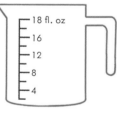

10 fl. oz   6 fl. oz

Score

Sticker

_____
5

What is the mass of each type of fruit?

.... lb

.... oz

.... oz

.... oz

Can you match the object to its approximate mass?

10 oz

2 oz

11 lb

$\frac{1}{1,000}$ oz

Convert these units:

8 oz = ... lb

2 lb = ... oz

24 oz = ... lb

$\frac{1}{4}$ lb = ... oz

1 t = ... lb

$1\frac{1}{2}$ lb = ... oz

Score

Sticker

_____
4

_____
10

37

Measuring time

Time is usually measured in seconds (s), minutes (min) and hours (hr).

In a **second** you could...

...sneeze.

60 seconds make a minute.

In a **minute** you could...

...lace up your shoes.

60 minutes make an hour.

In an **hour** you could...

...play a game.

Can you fill in the missing time?

Our relay team needs to finish the race in 1 minute. I ran for 15 seconds.

I ran for 20 seconds.

So I need to finish in .... seconds.

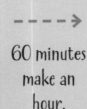

Work out who came 1st, 2nd and 3rd and give them medals from the sticker pages.

I finished the race in 28 minutes.

I finished in a quarter of an hour.

I finished in half an hour.

Which unit of time would you use to measure each race?

Seconds ....
Hours ....
Days ....

A

Marathon 26 mi

200 yd sprint

B

C

Tour de France 2,192 mi

You can measure time using clocks and timers.

A clock tells you what time of day it is by counting the hours since midnight (or noon).

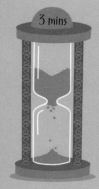

3 mins

A sand timer measures a fixed amount of time. When all the sand has fallen to the bottom, that time is up.

A stopwatch tells you how long has passed since you pressed 'start'.

hr min s
01: 30: 41

This competition has three events. How long did the whole competition take this athlete?

hr   min   s
.... : .... : ....

hr min s
01:00:00

hr min s
01:15:00

hr min s
00:45:00

winning time
hr   min   s
00:03:58

world record
hr   min   s
00:03:08

Use this space for working out.

How many seconds *faster* does she need to swim next time to beat the world record?

.... seconds

Temperature

Temperature means how hot or cold something is. You can measure it in degrees Fahrenheit (°F) using a thermometer.

The metric unit of temperature is degrees Celsius (°C). See how they compare on page 47.

This is a liquid thermometer.

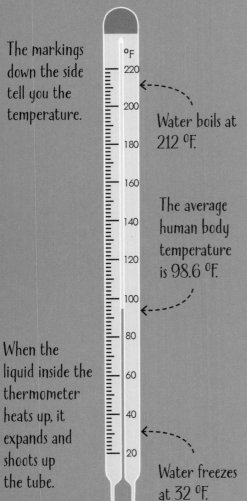

The markings down the side tell you the temperature.

Water boils at 212 °F.

The average human body temperature is 98.6 °F.

When the liquid inside the thermometer heats up, it expands and shoots up the tube.

Water freezes at 32 °F.

Choose the right temperature sticker for each picture below, and stick it on.

Can you make these thermometers show the right temperature?

It's 80 °F today.

It's dropped to 30 °F now.

Thermal imaging cameras create images based on heat. This allows photographers to take photos even in the dark. Color in this thermal image following the key, to show what the forest looks like through the camera.

Look at the thermal image and work out if these things are true or false.

Hooves are the hottest part of a deer's body.

TRUE / FALSE

Deer antlers are the same temperature all over.

TRUE / FALSE

The leaves all have a temperature of about 70 °F.

TRUE / FALSE

Measuring turns

Degrees (°) are the unit for measuring turns.

A clockwise turn means turning in the same direction as the hands on a clock.

A counter-clockwise turn means turning the other way.

If you turn all the way around, you'll have turned 360°.

Turning halfway is 180°.

A quarter turn is 90°.

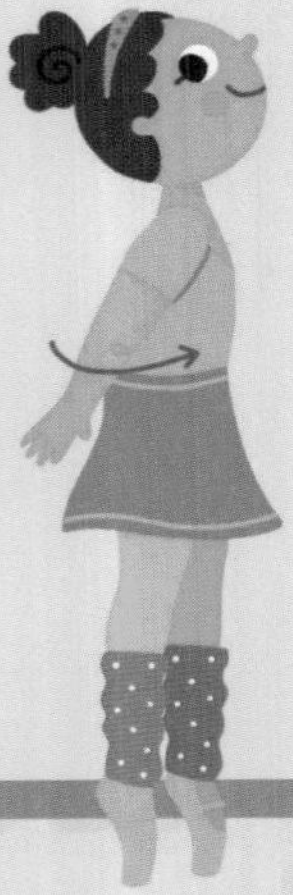

360° On paper, a 360° turn, known as an angle, looks like this.

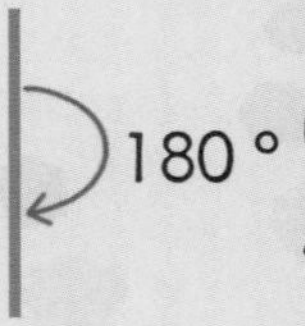

180° On paper, a 180° angle looks like this.

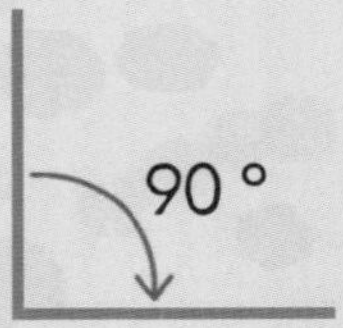

90° This is a 90° angle. It's also called a right angle.

Can you fill in how many degrees these dancers have turned counter-clockwise?

Start ....° Finish

Start ....° Finish

Can you trace this dancer's path across the room, following the instructions? Circle where he finishes.

1 Four steps forward and turn 90 ° degrees counter-clockwise

2 Two steps forward and turn 90 ° clockwise

3 Three steps forward and turn 360 °

4 Then two steps forward

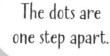

The dots are one step apart.

START

Metric units

These units are used all around the world, especially by scientists who need to be very precise.
The beginning of each unit's name is a clue as to whether it's a big or small unit.

Getting bigger

Biggest

Information stored by computers is measured in bytes.

Tera- makes a unit a trillion times bigger. --→ A **terabyte** is a trillion bytes. --→ 1 terabyte is enough to store several hundred thousand books.

Giga- makes a unit a billion times bigger. --→ A **gigabyte** is a billion bytes. --→ 1 gigabyte is enough to store about a thousand books.

Mega- makes a unit a million times bigger. --→ A **megabyte** is a million bytes. --→ 1 megabyte is enough to store about one book.

Kilo- makes a unit a thousand times bigger. --→ A **kilobyte** is a thousand bytes. --→ 1 kilobyte is about the size of a text message.

Getting smaller

Centi- makes a unit a hundred times smaller. --→ A **centimeter** is a hundredth of a meter. (1 meter = 1.09 yard) --→ A shield bug is about 1 centimeter long.

Milli- makes a unit a thousand times smaller. --→ A **millimeter** is a thousandth of a meter. --→ An ant is about 5 millimeters long.

Micro- makes a unit a million times smaller. --→ A **micrometer** is a millionth of a meter. --→ An eyelash is about 90 micrometers wide.

Nano- makes a unit a billion times smaller. --→ A **nanometer** is a billionth of a meter. --→ The wall of a bubble is about 10 nanometers wide.

Smallest

Can you identify these things following the flow chart? The pictures are not shown to scale.

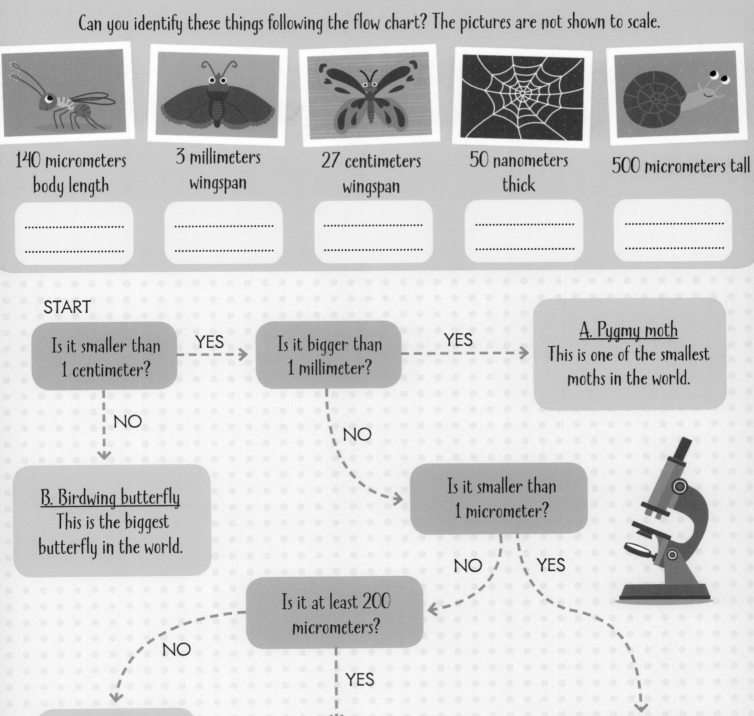

140 micrometers body length

3 millimeters wingspan

27 centimeters wingspan

50 nanometers thick

500 micrometers tall

....
....

....
....

....
....

....
....

....
....

START

Is it smaller than 1 centimeter? —— YES → Is it bigger than 1 millimeter? —— YES → **A. Pygmy moth** This is one of the smallest moths in the world.

NO ↓

B. Birdwing butterfly This is the biggest butterfly in the world.

Is it bigger than 1 millimeter? —— NO → Is it smaller than 1 micrometer?

Is it smaller than 1 micrometer? — NO → Is it at least 200 micrometers?

Is it smaller than 1 micrometer? — YES →

Is it at least 200 micrometers? — NO → **C. Fairy fly** This insect is the smallest ever found. It's too small to see with the naked eye.

Is it at least 200 micrometers? — YES → **D. Micro snail** This is the smallest snail yet found. It's so small, it can fit through the eye of a needle.

E. Thinnest spider thread It's spun by the lace weaver spider.

Converting units

These pages will help you compare metric
and customary units, and convert
between different kinds of units.

Metric units

Length

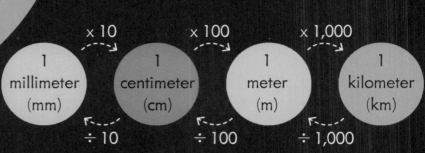

	×10 →	×100 →	×1,000 →
1 millimeter (mm)	1 centimeter (cm)	1 meter (m)	1 kilometer (km)
	÷10 ←	÷100 ←	÷1,000 ←

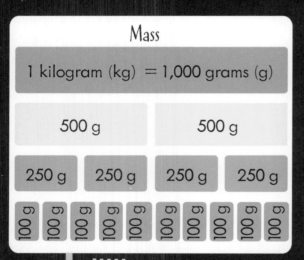

Mass

1 kilogram (kg) = 1,000 grams (g)

500 g	500 g

250 g	250 g	250 g	250 g

| 100 g | 100 g | 100 g | 100 g | 100 g | 100 g | 100 g | 100 g | 100 g | 100 g |

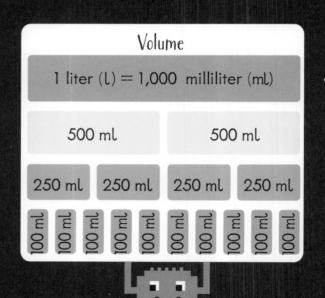

Volume

1 liter (L) = 1,000 milliliter (mL)

500 ml	500 ml

250 ml	250 ml	250 ml	250 ml

| 100 ml | 100 ml | 100 ml | 100 ml | 100 ml | 100 ml | 100 ml | 100 ml | 100 ml | 100 ml |

Converting between metric and customary units

Here's how some metric and customary units compare.

Roughly you can say:

2.5 cm = 1 in

1 m = 3 ft

5 km = 3 mi

30 g = 1 oz

Or more accurately:

1 cm = 0.39 in
1 in = 2.54 cm

1 m = 3.28 ft
1 ft = 0.30 m

1 km = 0.62 mi
1 mi = 1.61 km

10 g = 0.35 oz
1 oz = 28.35 g

These units are used in the United States, where they are known as customary units, and some other countries around the world. You might also see them in old books and road signs.

Length

yard		
foot	foot	foot
6 inches	6 inches	6 inches	6 inches	6 inches	6 inches

1 mile = 1,760 yards

Volume

gallon			
quart	quart	quart	quart
pint	pint	pint	pint	pint	pint	pint	pint
10 fl. oz	10 fl. oz	10 fl. oz	10 fl. oz	10 fl. oz	10 fl. oz	10 fl. oz	10 fl. oz	10 fl. oz	10 fl. oz	10 fl. oz	10 fl. oz	10 fl. oz	10 fl. oz	10 fl. oz	10 fl. oz

Pints and fluid ounces (fl. oz) are slightly different in the US and UK.

Mass

pound			
$\frac{1}{2}$ pound		$\frac{1}{2}$ pound	
$\frac{1}{4}$ pound	$\frac{1}{4}$ pound	$\frac{1}{4}$ pound	$\frac{1}{4}$ pound
ounce ounce ounce ounce	ounce ounce ounce ounce	ounce ounce ounce ounce	ounce ounce ounce ounce

1 stone = 14 pounds

This thermometer shows how degrees Fahrenheit and Celsius compare.

°F / °C

Boiling point of water → 200 / 100
90
180 / 80
160 / 70
140 / 60
120 / 50
40
100 / 30
80 / 20
60 / 10
Freezing point of water → 40 / 0
20 / -10

1 kg = 2 pounds

1 l = 2 pints

100 ml = 3 fl. oz

1 kg = 2.20 pounds
1 pound = 0.45 kg

1 l = 2.11 pints
1 pint = 0.47 l

100 ml = 3.38 fl. oz
1 fl. oz = 29.57 ml

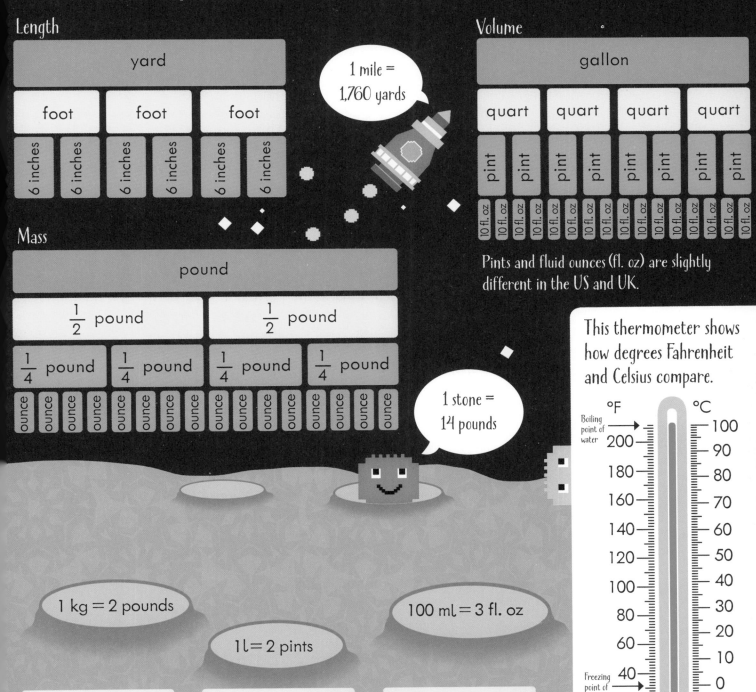

47

Can you write what each of these things is used to measure?

....

....

....

....

....

Score   Sticker

5

Can you make these thermometers show the right temperature?

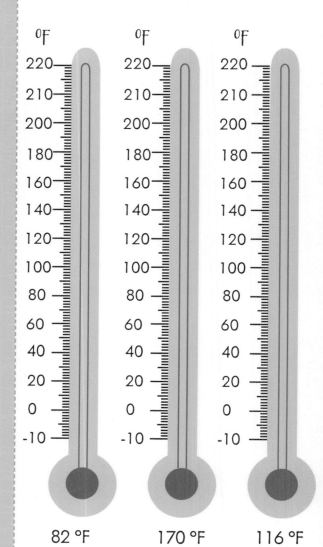

82 °F   170 °F   116 °F

Score   Sticker

3

Circle all the right angles in these shapes.

Look at the shapes below. For each pair, how much does the shape on the left need to turn clockwise, to match the shape on the right... a quarter turn or a half turn?

....

....

....

Score

Sticker

_____

6

Can you label these things 1 to 4, with 1 taking the shortest time, and 4 taking the longest?

.... brushing teeth

.... watching a movie

.... growing tomatoes
          from seeds

.... blinking

Can you complete the additions?

Tip: 60 s = 1 min
60 min = 1 hr

20 s + 30 s + ... = 1 min

10 s + 10 s + ... = 1 min

15 s + 25 s + ... = 1 min

30 min + 15 min + ... = 1 hr

45 min + 5 min + ... = 1 hr

Score

Sticker

_____

9

Art gallery

Color in the shapes in this painting by matching the area of each shape to the color in the key.

On the painting, a square of 1 in² looks like this:

KEY

1 in²:

2 in²:

3 in²:

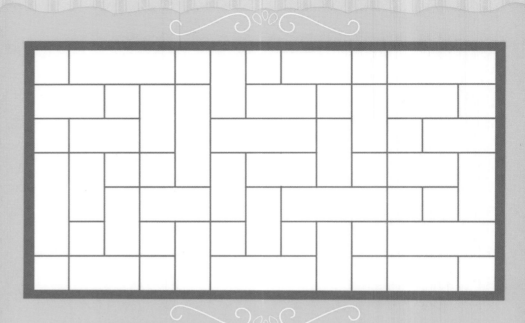

Answer the questions below, using the ruler from page five to help you.

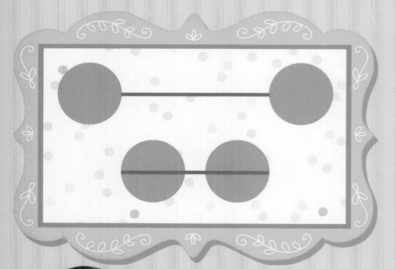

Is the top horizontal line longer than the bottom one?

Yes / No

Does the flower on the right have a bigger middle?

Yes / No

In this picture, the daisy has the smallest stem. The stem of the rose should be taller than the tulip, but smaller than the purple iris. Using the stickers, can you put the flowers on the stems?

Can you circle the piece of fruit in this painting that would have a mass of more than 2 lb.

Artists use grids to help them scale up their sketches. Can you copy this sketch onto the bigger canvas, one square at a time, estimating where each line should go?

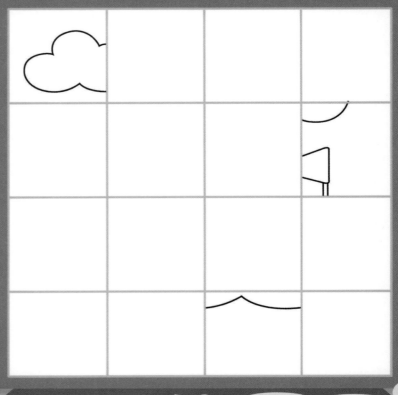

Ocean crossing

Solve the puzzles, then trace the ship's route back to port.

The sailors spot a seal after half an hour. Which is the same as...

30 minutes

60 minutes

You can only see a tenth, or 1,000 in³, of this iceberg. What's the volume of the whole iceberg?

10,000 in³

1,000,000 in³

10 in³

This young narwhal is 9 ft long from tip to tail. Roughly how long do you think just its tusk is?

5 ft

600 yd

3 ft

2 ft

The sailors want to sail around Icy Island. What's its perimeter?

700 yd

100 yd

200 yd

50 yd

100 yd

250 yd

This thermometer shows the temperature during the day. If it's 20 °F colder at night, what will it say then?

°F
40
30
20
10
0
-10
-20
-30

15 °F

-15 °F

How many degrees did these penguins turn?

90°

32 oz

The sailors collect 4 lb of edible seaweed. Yum! That's the same as...

3 lb

180°

64 oz

This puffin has caught 12 fish. Each one has a mass of 4 oz. What's the total mass?

2 ½ lb

This sailor dives down to explore. She has enough air to last 60 minutes. That's the same as...

4 oz

1 hour

Oh it's good to be home!

6 hours

The ship sailed 1,000 miles every week for 5 weeks. How many miles was that?

5,000 mi

Monster measuring

Can you match each monster to its cup of tea?

I need 2 pt.

I just want 1 fl. oz.

Half a cup please.

2 qt for me.

I need 1 cup.

How much tea do the tea monsters drink in total?

You can use this space for working out.

This monster has used 15 gallons of water in its bath.

How much water do you think this monster has used?

Can you find the right sign for each monster from the sticker pages, and stick it on the monster's door?

I need to nap for less than half an hour.

I need to nap for more than 40 minutes.

Each monster is juggling a set of weights adding up to 1 lb.

Each of my weights is .... oz.

Each of my weights is .... oz.

Match each thing to the unit you would use to measure it.

ounces   pints   pounds

Chocolate

Soup

Monster pumpkin

Can you award sticker prizes to each monster following the key?
You can use your ruler from page five to help you.

PRIZES

Spike polish

Longest spike

Widest eye

Tallest monster

Longest fang

World records

Can you stick the names of the world's highest mountains onto these posters?

29,028 ft

Even higher than K2

28,251 ft
Taller than
Kanchenjunga

28,169 ft
Smaller than
Everest and K2

These animals make the longest journeys in the world. Put a sticker of each animal by its route on the map.

Humpback whale: 13,700 mi

Sooty shearwater: 40,400 mi

Arctic tern: 44,100 mi

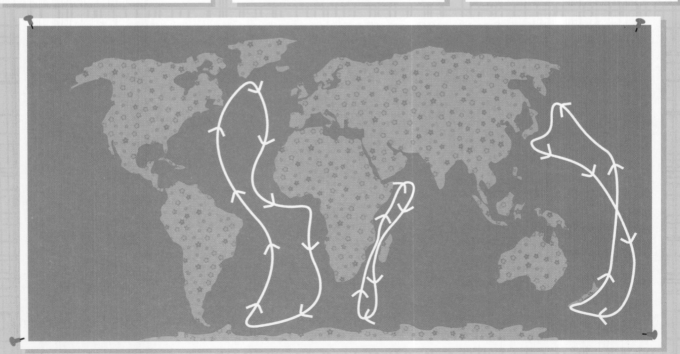

These postcards show the hottest and coldest places in the world.
Stick thermometers showing the right temperatures by each one.

132 °F

Greetings from
Death Valley
USA

118 °F

Sunny Aziziyah
Libya

-115 °F

The South Pole

Wish you
were here!

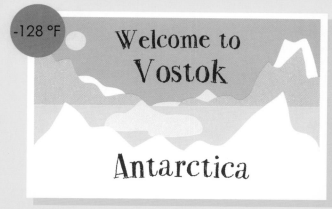

-128 °F

Welcome to
Vostok

Antarctica

These are the four biggest lakes in the world. Can you number them from biggest to smallest, with 1 being the biggest and 4 the smallest?

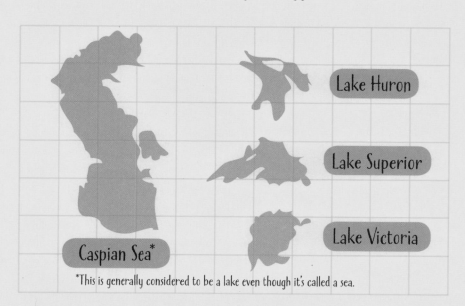

Lake Huron

Lake Superior

Lake Victoria

Caspian Sea*

*This is generally considered to be a lake even though it's called a sea.

Circle the heaviest hailstone ever recorded.

30 oz

32 oz

$2\frac{1}{4}$ lb

Answers
4-5 Comparing things

The bike on the right is about twice as wide as the bike on the left.

I'm 2 times taller.

I'm 3 times as tall.

I'm $1\frac{1}{2}$ times as tall.

6-7 Measuring length

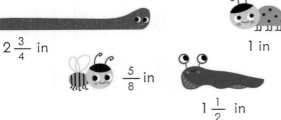

$2\frac{3}{4}$ in

1 in

$\frac{5}{8}$ in

$1\frac{1}{2}$ in

Shortest twig: $1\frac{3}{8}$ in

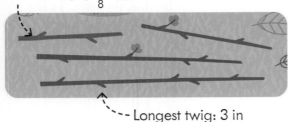

Longest twig: 3 in

The caterpillar is 2 inches long.
One week later it is $2\frac{3}{4}$ inches long.

The frog on the left jumped about 3 inches and the frog on the right jumped about $1\frac{1}{2}$ inches.

8-9 Longer distances

A sailing trip around the world: miles
Length of a beach towel: feet
Height of a beach umbrella: feet

The small sail is about $\frac{1}{4}$ smaller. So it is about 3 yards high.

Sandcastle competition:
A: 6 ft
B: 8 ft
C: 7 ft
So B is the longest.

This is the right board. It is 8 ft tall.

In half the time, the runners have run about half the distance. So that's about half a mile.

10-11 From one unit to another

1 yd

1 ft

12 in

4 yd

6 ft

2 yd

12 ft

3 ft

The gold and silver goblet are the same height. The emerald and ruby plate are the same width.

The queen is right. She owns 120 in or 10 ft of necklaces.

The princess's route:
$50 + 50 + 50 + 50 + 50 + 50 + 100 + 200 + 50 + 50 + 50 + 100 = 850$ yd
That's less than a mile.

The pigeon on the left is going to the castle.
2 mi = 3,520 yd
The pigeon in the middle going to the house .
600 ft = 200 yd
The pigeon on the right is going to the inn.
$\frac{1}{2}$ mi = 200 yd

12–13 More practice

The saddle on the left is about twice as high as the block, or $2 \times 2 = 4$ ft.
The saddle on the right is about 3 times as high as the block, or $1 \times 3 = 3$ ft.

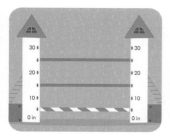

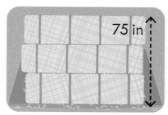

75 in

Jump A: green rider   Jump B: blue rider
Jump C: red rider

Lengths of the jumps: A) 3 ft   B) $1\frac{1}{2}$ ft   C) $3\frac{1}{2}$ ft

14–15 Quick quiz

The lines, from longest to shortest: C, D, B, A, E.

Matching measuring devices to their description: 1C, 2A, 3B.

Units from top to bottom: miles, feet, inches, inches.

1 yd = 3 ft
1 ft = 12 in
9 ft = 3 yd
48 in = 4 ft
$\frac{1}{3}$ yd = 1 ft

2 ft = 24 in
10 yd = 30 ft
1 mi = 1,760 yd
$\frac{1}{2}$ ft = 6 in

16–17 Perimeter

The farmers need:
$5 + 10 + 5 + 10 = 30$ yd of wire.
So the farmer on the right is correct.

Pumpkin patch: $2 + 3 + 2 + 3 = 10$ yd
Carrot patch: $1 + 3 + 1 + 3 = 8$ yd
Cabbage patch: $2 + 5 + 2 + 5 = 14$ yd

The perimeter of the sheep pen:
$25 + 15 + 25 + 15 = 80$ yd
So the middle dog has just run around the perimeter.

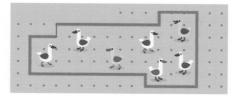

The farmer needs 38 yd of fencing for the goose pen.

18–19 Area

The red rocket has an area of about 6 in².
The blue rocket has an area of about 8 in².

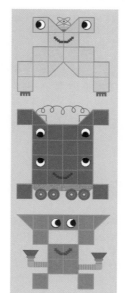

Planet deliveries:

The spaceship has won 3 red badges and 4 blue badges.

20-21 More area

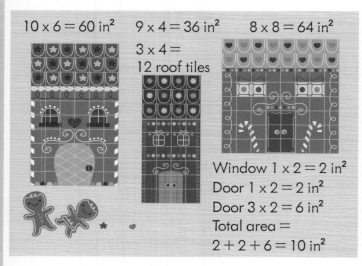

$10 \times 6 = 60$ in² $\quad 9 \times 4 = 36$ in² $\quad 8 \times 8 = 64$ in²

$3 \times 4 = 12$ roof tiles

Window $1 \times 2 = 2$ in²
Door $1 \times 2 = 2$ in²
Door $3 \times 2 = 6$ in²
Total area = $2 + 2 + 6 = 10$ in²

The area of candy before the bakers cut it:
$4 \times 7 = 28$ in²

Roughly $3 \times 4 = 12$ gingerbread men can be cut from the tray of gingerbread.

$7 \times 3 = 21$ in² $\quad 5 \times 3 = 15$ in² $\quad 7 \times 3 = 21$ in²

The square house on the left-hand page has an area twice as big as this one.

$8 \times 4 = 32$ in²

$21 + 15 + 21 = 57$ in²

22-23 Quick quiz

Shape A: $4 + 4 + 4 + 4 = 16$ in
Shape B: $7 + 2.5 + 2 + 3 + 3 + 3 + 2 + 2.5 = 25$ in

Perimeter of the field: $25 + 50 + 25 + 50 = 150$ yd

Perimeter of the square vegetable patch:
$5 + 5 + 5 + 5 = 20$ yd

Perimeter of the rectangular field:
$100 + 100 + 50 + 50 = 300$ yd

Area:
A) 10 in² B) 10 in² C) 11 in²
D) About 10 in² E) 10 in²

24-25 Capacity and volume

The honey jar has the smallest capacity. The strawberry jam jar has the biggest.

The mouse stole a cube from the right-hand pile of cheese.

From left to right, the blocks will last: 3 days, 4 days and 2 days.

16 cubes = 16 in³ $\qquad$ 20 cubes = 20 in³

26-27 Volume of liquids

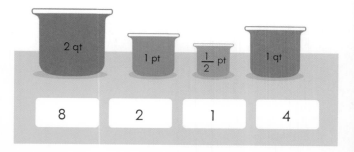

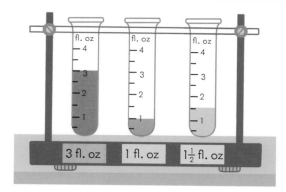

3 fl. oz 1 fl. oz $1\frac{1}{2}$ fl. oz

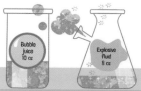

Fizz reaction:

12 fl. oz 7 fl. oz

13 fl. oz 6 fl. oz

28–29 More volumes

The worker needs to add half a cup of strawberry juice.

The machine can fill five cartons of kiwi juice.

The worker needs four bottles of blueberry juice.

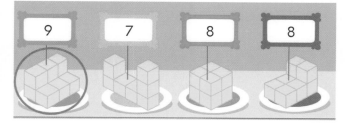

9 7 8 8

About two ladles will fill the green container.

The right hand mango container has the most mango juice.

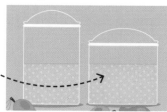

Rainbow juice:

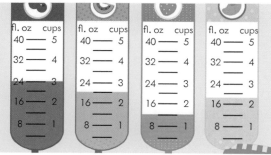

30–31 Measuring mass

An eagle can carry about 4 lb of fish in its claws.
A brown bear has a mass of about 1,000 lb.
A rabbit has a mass of about 4 lb.

Camper's stew:

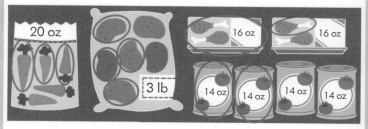

20 oz 3 lb 16 oz 16 oz
14 oz 14 oz 14 oz 14 oz

The cable car is strong enough to carry the whole family.

32–33 Using scales

The baker needs 12 oz of flour, 14 oz of cherries and 7 oz of chocolate.

From left to right, the piles of raspberries have a mass of $\frac{1}{2}$ lb, 1 lb and $\frac{1}{4}$ lb.

You could make 6 croissants from this pile of dough.

The weights need to add up to 16 oz. There is more than one way to do this.

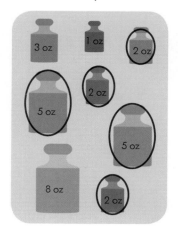

3 oz 1 oz 2 oz
5 oz 2 oz
 5 oz
8 oz 2 oz

1 tart: 1 lb 1 eclair: 4 oz
4 tarts: 4 lb 10 eclair: 40 oz or $2\frac{1}{2}$ lb

34 – 35 More practice

Lion cub weigh-in:
Ari: 8 lb   Leo: 5 lb   Fluffy: 7 lb

Elephant mass:

The top monkey is $1\frac{1}{2}$ lb or 24 oz lighter.

The baby giraffe has a mass of about 1,000 lb.

The hippo record has the wrong mass written on it. Hippos have a mass of about 3,300 lb.

The left-hand pair of scales: 5 meerkats.
The right-hand pair of scales: 3 meerkats.

14 lb   196 lb   14 oz

---

36 – 37 Quick quiz

4) cup 5) spoon 2) bottle 1) saucepan 3) bowl

A) 6 in³ B) 7 in³ C) 7 in³

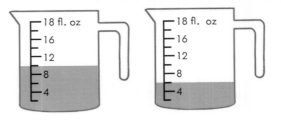

watermelon: 12 lb   blueberries: 6 oz
mangoes: 18 oz   pineapple: 36 oz

necklace: 2 oz   feather: 1/1000 oz
pumpkin: 11 lb   jar of jam: 10 oz

$8 \text{ oz} = \frac{1}{2} \text{ lb}$ $\frac{1}{4} \text{ lb} = 4 \text{ oz}$
$2 \text{ lb} = 32 \text{ oz}$ $1 \text{ t} = 2,000 \text{ lb}$
$24 \text{ oz} = 1\frac{1}{2} \text{ lb}$ $1\frac{1}{2} \text{ lb} = 24 \text{ oz}$

---

38 – 39 Measuring time

The last relay racer needs to finish in 25 seconds.

Race posters:
Seconds: B
Hours: A
Days: C

The whole competition took:
1 hr + 1 hr + 15 min + 45 min = 3 hr

The swimmer needs to swim 50 seconds faster to *match* the world record, or 51 seconds faster to *beat* it.

---

40 – 41 Temperature

194 °F   99 °F   50 °F

From left to right:
FALSE   FALSE   TRUE

42-43 Measuring turns

The dancer on the left has turned 180°.
The dancer on the right has turned 90°.

The dancer on the left is making a 180° angle with her legs. The dancer on the right is making a 90° angle with his legs.

The dancer on the left has turned 180°.
The dancer on the right has turned 90°.

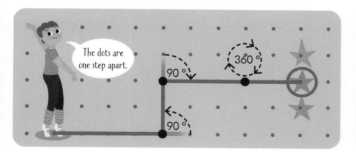

The dots are one step apart.

44-45 Very big to very small

The things from left to right: fairy fly, pygmy moth, birdwing butterfly, thinnest spider thread, micro snail.

48-49 Quick quiz

Length

Time

Temperature

Mass

Volume of liquids

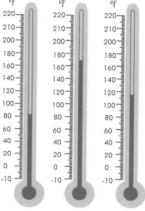

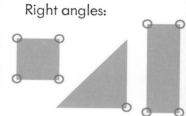

Right angles:

From top to bottom the shapes have turned: a half turn, a quarter turn, a quarter turn.

Shortest to longest:
2) brushing teeth   3) watching a movie
4) growing tomatoes from seed   1) blinking

20 s + 30 s + 10 s = 1 min
10 s + 10 s + 40 s = 1 min
15 s + 25 s + 20 s = 1 min
30 min + 15 min + 15 min = 1 hr
45 min + 5 min + 10 min = 1 hr

50-51 Art gallery

The two lines are the same length. The two gray circles are the same size too. They only look different because the red shapes around them trick your brain.

52-53 Ocean crossing

54-55 Monster measuring

The monsters drink $13\frac{1}{2}$ cups and 1 fl. oz of tea.

The monster has used about 30 gallons of water.

The monster on the left has the yellow sign and the monster on the right has the blue sign.

The yellow monster's weights have a mass of 4 oz each. The orange monster's weights have a mass of 2 oz each.

Chocolate: ounces

Soup: pints

Monster pumpkin: pounds

56-57 World records

The mountain posters from left to right: Everest, K2 and Kanchenjunga.

The animal journeys from left to right: arctic tern, humpback whale, sooty shearwater.

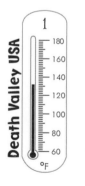

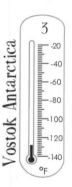
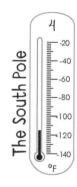

List of lakes, from biggest to smallest:
1. Caspian Sea
2. Superior
3. Victoria
4. Huron

The bottom hailstone has the biggest mass.

Edited by Rosie Dickins   Managing designer: Zoe Wray
Additional design by Sarah Vince   American Editor: Carrie Armstrong

First published in 2018 by Usborne Publishing Ltd., 83-85 Saffron Hill, London, EC1N 8RT, England. www.usborne.com Copyright © 2018 Usborne Publishing Ltd.
The name Usborne and the devices ♀ ♁ are Trade Marks of Usborne Publishing Ltd. All rights reserved. No part of this publication may be reproduced, stored in a retrieval system, or transmitted in any form or by any means, electronic, mechanical, photocopying, recording or otherwise, without the prior permission of the publisher. AE.

Comparing

Put the right bow tie and hat onto the dog and clown on page 4.

Measuring length

Stick these flowers in the planter on page 7.

Longer distances

Award the ribbon to the longest sandcastle on page 9.

Stick these riders onto the horses on page 13.

More practice

Use these hay bales to finish the jump on page 12.

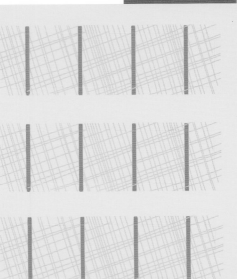

Area

Help the spaceship on page 19 complete its mission by sticking these stickers on the planets.

Give these badges to the spaceship following the rules on page 19.

More area

Decorate the gingerbread house on page 20 with these windows and this door.

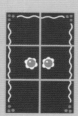

Capacity

Stick these cookie jars onto the shelves on page 24.

Volume

Add these labels to the flasks on page 27.

Explosive
fluid
8 oz

Bubble
juice
10 oz

More practice

Stick these kiwi juice cartons onto the conveyor belt on page 28.

Using scales

Stick the right number of croissants onto the tray on page 33.

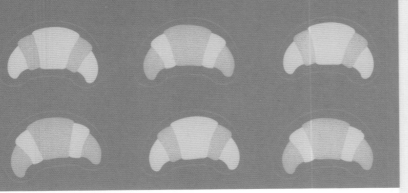

Temperature

Match these temperatures to the right object or person on page 40.

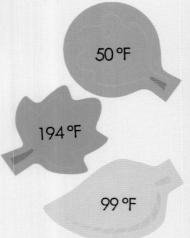

50 °F

194 °F

99 °F

More practice

Add these baby meerkats to the scales on page 35.

Stick the labels of these animals onto the buckets of food on page 35.

Art gallery

Add these flowers to the vase in the painting on page 51.

Time

Give these medals to the competitors on page 38.

1st

3rd

2nd

Monsters

Stick these signs onto the monsters' doors on page 54.

Wake me up in 20 mins

Wake me up in $\frac{3}{4}$ of an hour